Specially made for Moms

BECAUSE MOMS ARE SO SPECIAL

A GIFT COLORING BOOK FOR MOMs

Dedicated to my Mom and all the Moms in the world
who keep on working so hard just for their child .

You are treasured and loved.
Your selflessness, your patience, kindness and gentleness
are the most precious treasures of all.
Only moms knows what is best for her child.
You may say no sometimes,
you may not give in with us all the time,
and at first we may not understand
because of being a child
but you know that in the end
we'll realize that everything you do
is for the love you have for us.

Mom,
These coloring pages are specially
made for you. Color them and keep
them safe with you. A reminder that
somebody out here is always
thinking of you!

Mom, I thank you for the love, I thank God everyday. That I am given this life to cherish from day to day.

Always so happy that you are my family. You never failed to show me that in this life there is a

beautiful Mom

for me to cherish

everyday

There are no words to express
how grateful I am
that you are my mom.
My life is so blessed
because you are my mom.
I feel so complete and compensated
because of you mom.
I admire you,
I treasure your love,
You are the best of the best.
I love you mom!

Thank you mom, For the times when I was burdensome,

You never gave up one me. For the times when I never listened,

You never gave up on me. For the times when I stay away,

thought I could do it by my own Still... you never gave up on me.

For the times I thought I was right, For the times I that forget that you

were everything I had when no one else are around.

I am not perfect, I may not say it a lot,

But I do hope you know

that deep inside my heart

Your name is always

carved!

MOM
You are great

You are my hero. You are my knight. You are my Bestfriend. You are my light.
I love you mom.
I will treasure this for life!

You brought me into this
world
You took care of me 'til I'm old
You gave me food, You gave me shelter, You gave
me everything you could ever give.
Without fear, Without pause,
Without hesitation, Without limitation.
Never asked for something in return.
All you wanted was me
to become somebody someday. And be the best
person you wished I would be..

I love you mom, You are the best!

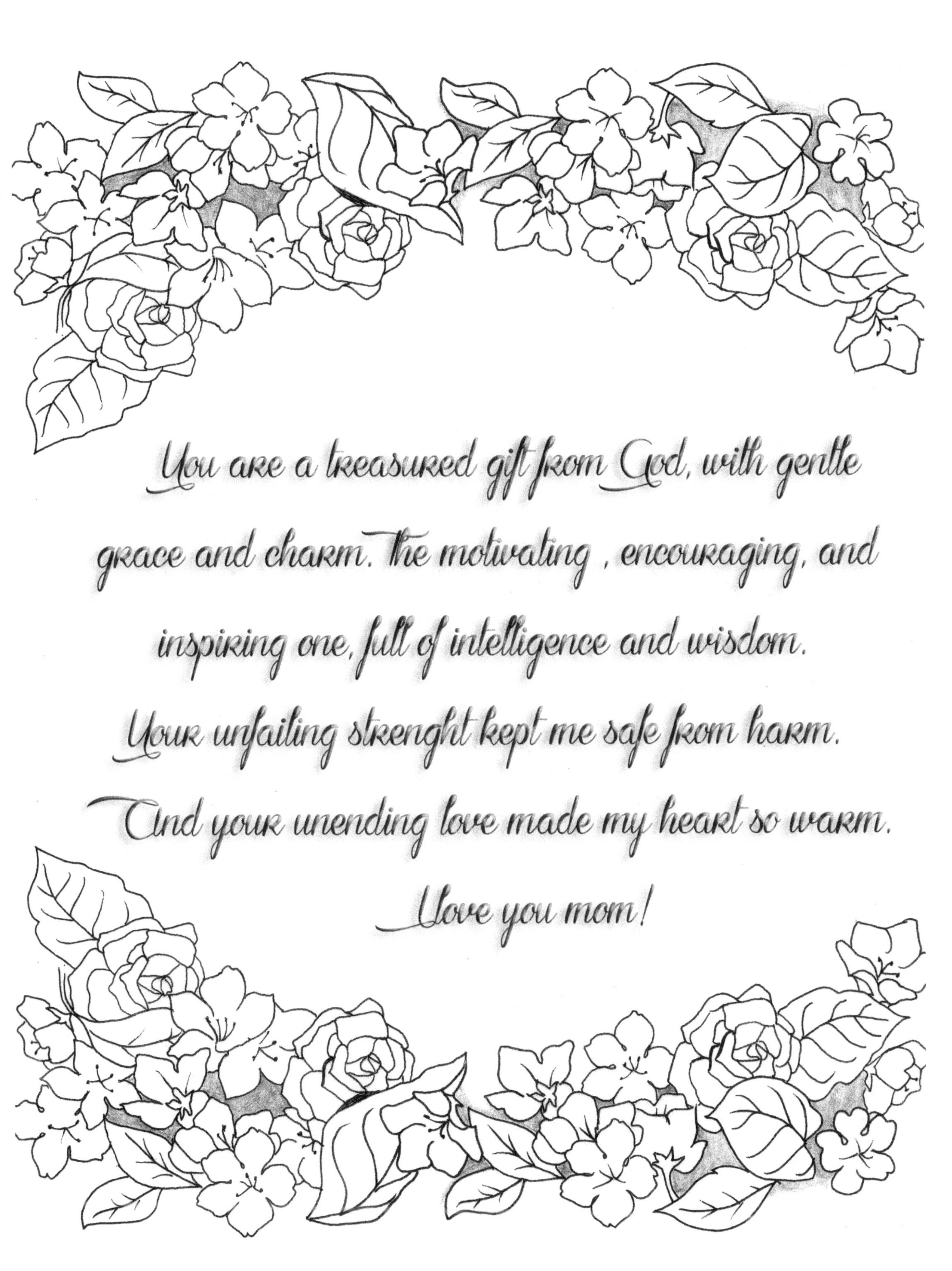

You are a treasured gift from God, with gentle
grace and charm. The motivating, encouraging, and
inspiring one, full of intelligence and wisdom.
Your unfailing strenght kept me safe from harm.
And your unending love made my heart so warm.
I love you mom!

Mom,
I Sometimes forget
to tell you
How awesome you are to
me
But please
don't ever forget
that here in my heart
you the reason
that it beats!
I love you
mom!

Please keep this tiny
little keepsake
I have given you away,
A reminder that
no matter how far you think
I might be,
In times when
I needed to be away,
Always remember you are in
my heart everyday...

I love
My loving mom

Your love is endless , Your love is pure ,
It never judges and is always sure.

You are kindhearted you never failed to prove ,
That I am your most precious one ,
You treasured me like gold.
You promised me one thing
and I promise the same ,
That I will love you forever ,
And forever I will be the same

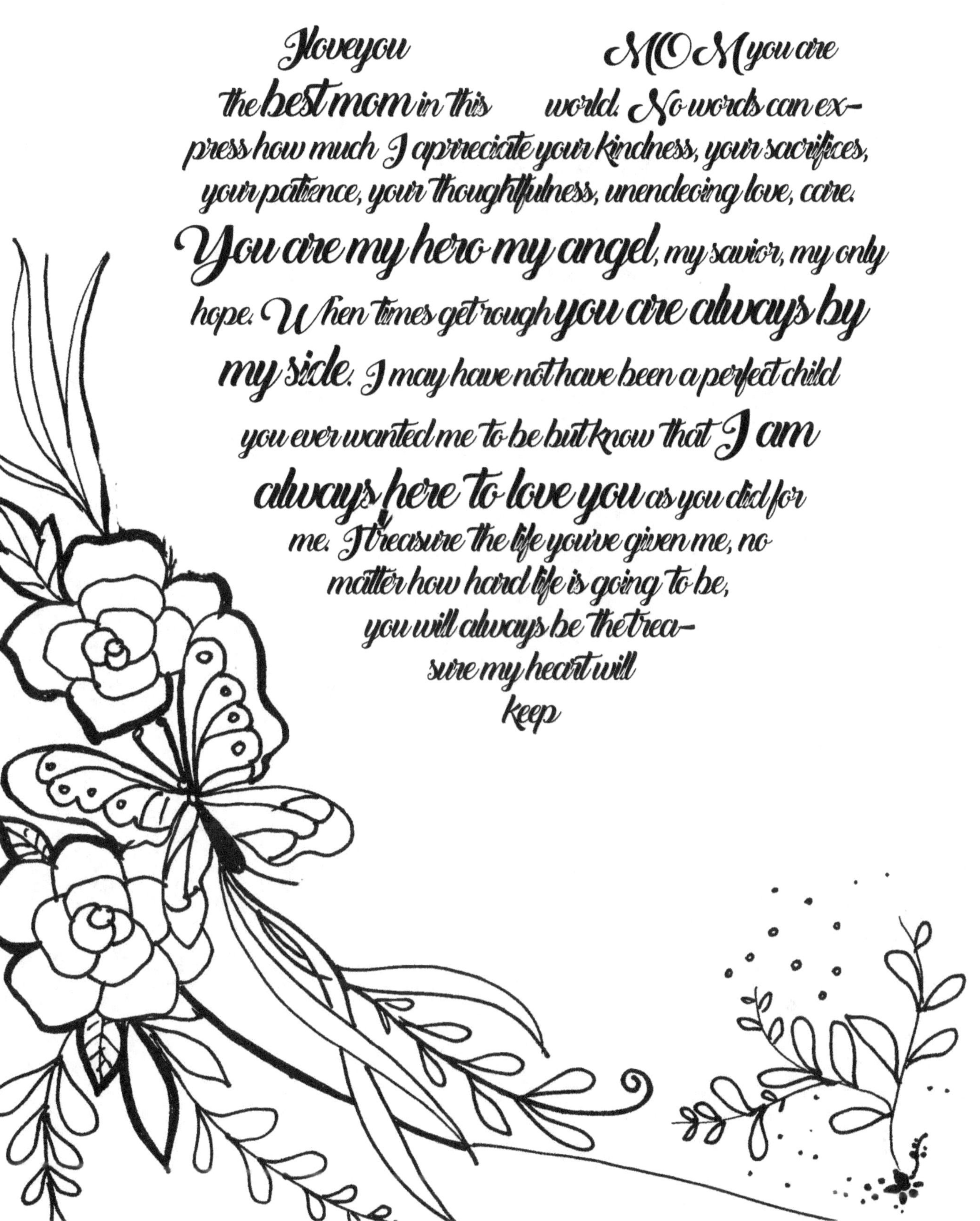

I love you MOM you are the best mom in this world. No words can express how much I appreciate your kindness, your sacrifices, your patience, your thoughtfulness, unendearing love, care. You are my hero my angel, my savior, my only hope. When times get rough you are always by my side. I may have not have been a perfect child you ever wanted me to be but know that I am always here to love you as you did for me. I treasure the life you've given me, no matter how hard life is going to be, you will always be the treasure my heart will keep

Thank you Mom
For being the one
that never stopped loving
never stopped caring,

The one I can always count on
When everything has gone wrong
Your love is the greatest
treasure I have...

I Love you from
all of my heart!

Thank you mom,
No matter what we've been
through, No matter how selfish
and troublesome I am to you.
You never said you had enough,
But even if you did say,
Your actions don't do the same way.
I love you mom,
Thank you for loving me!

Saying thank you will never be

enough!

For you have sacrificed more than enough.

Gave up eveything and gave me all that you have.

Worked hard to give your precious child a

better life than what you had...

Thank you mom, thanks a lot...

For you are the reason that in this life

I am around

MOM

You are the Beautiful butterfly

THAT MAKES THE FLOWERS SMILE

Mom,
this is specially made for you!
I love you!

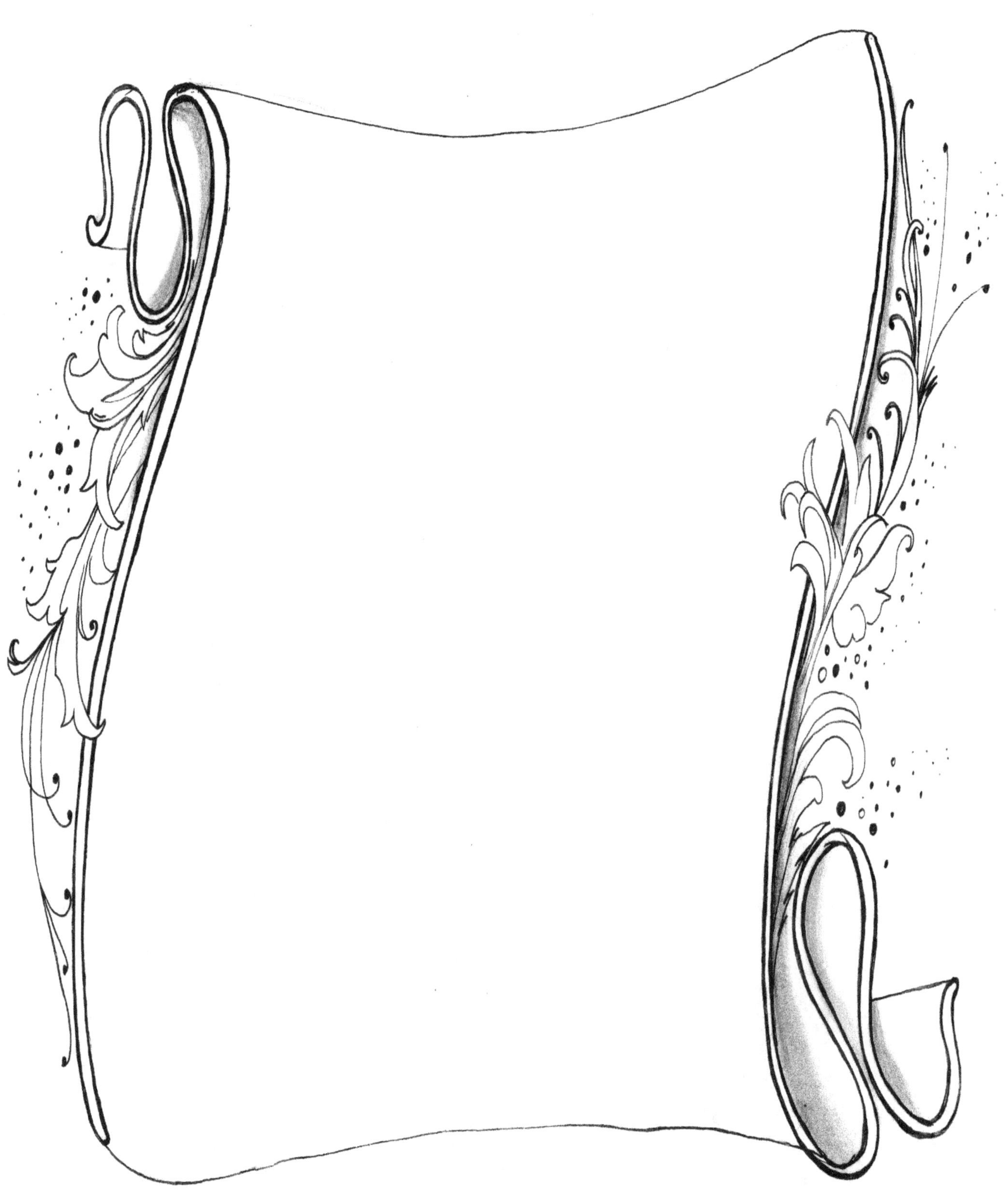